## BRITAIN IN OLD PHOTOGRAPHS

# SHREWSBURY

## A Second Selection

*DAVID TRUMPER*

ALAN SUTTON PUBLISHING LIMITED

Alan Sutton Publishing Limited
Phoenix Mill · Far Thrupp · Stroud
Gloucestershire · GL5 2BU

First published 1995

Cover photographs: (front) Frankwell in flood,
c. 1947; (back) Abbey Foregate, c. 1920.
Title page picture: Abbey Foregate, c. 1842.

British Library Cataloguing in Publication Data.
A catalogue record for this book is available from
the British Library.

ISBN 0–7509–1136–0

Typeset in 9/10 Sabon.
Typesetting and origination by
Alan Sutton Publishing Limited.
Printed in Great Britain by
Hartnolls, Bodmin, Cornwall.

> To Wendy, for twenty-five years

Frankwell, c. 1890. The suburb of Frankwell still possesses some of the finest examples of timber-framed houses in the town. This pair was built in the early part of the seventeenth century and has many features which are distinctive to Shrewsbury. The most striking features of the building on the left are the bays which project for over 3 ft. The cottage beyond the main buildings, with the sign at the first-floor window, is a small inn known as The Old House which was run by Henry Fallows, who is listed as a beer retailer. It was first recorded in 1883 and de-licensed on 4 October 1924. On the right we get a glimpse of the Fellmongers Hall, and beyond that the tall, brick building known in the last century as the Sweep's Lodging House.

# Contents

# Introduction

The suburbs of Shrewsbury are unique. In recent years, a growing fascination to study, explore and research the outskirts has developed, shedding light on the history of the buildings, industries and communities which have evolved there.

The town of Shrewsbury developed within the defensive horseshoe loop of the River Severn, and, by the time of the Norman conquest, a prosperous and well-organized community was thriving. The first communities to live outside the town were huddled near the main gateways or fords for quick entry in times of trouble. The suburbs of Abbey Foregate and Coleham are of Saxon origin, while Frankwell and Castle Foregate were settled soon after 1066.

The name Foregate describes land situated in front of a town gate. So Abbey Foregate refers to the land occupied by The Abbey in the east, and Castle Foregate refers to the district north of the town. It is suggested that Frankwell derived its name from an old French word meaning 'free town', a commercial area outside the jurisdiction of Shrewsbury. Alternatively, some sources say that forty-five Frenchmen arrived in the town shortly after the Conquest, and set up their own community, naming it Frankville. Coleham was recorded as Colneham, 'hamm' referring to land near the river, and 'Cole' or 'Colne' possibly being a personal name or some physical feature.

Abbey Foregate developed around the Benedictine Abbey of St Peter and St Paul, founded by Roger de Montgomery in 1083. This suburb, under the control of the abbot, was independent of the town. Disputes often arose between the governing bodies over land rights and the grinding of corn. A large community grew up to the north of the abbey, on land rented from the monastery, the people relying greatly on domestic work from the abbey. This left the abbot and the monks free to concentrate on religious affairs and administration. The abbey flourished for nearly four hundred years, having its own market place and fairs, until its dissolution in 1540. The suburb was finally united with the town under the charter of Elizabeth I in 1586. After the dissolution, it was hoped that the abbey could be converted into a college or free school, but the property was sold to William Langley, a local tailor. Many of the buildings were destroyed, some of the stone being used in the construction of Whitehall. The pleasure gardens to the south and east of the church were created by Henry Powis in about 1743.

The suburbs grew out of a need to develop certain industries away from the more crowded areas of the town, owing to the dreadful odours given off in some of the processes. Most of these trades dealt with the handling of animal skins. There were a number of skinners based in the four main suburbs, and tanning was carried out on a large scale, especially in Frankwell. As well as processing the raw material, there were craftsmen who would manufacture the finished product. Several shoemakers lived in Abbey Foregate, Frankwell and Coleham, and a number of glovers are mentioned in Castle Foregate. These trades continued for several hundred years. In Frankwell, the Fellmongers Hall was erected in the sixteenth century to process the fells (the sheepskins) brought in from Wales. Other trades carried out in the suburbs included brewing, dyeing and the making of pots and pans in Coleham.

By the seventeenth century, a great deal of trade was being brought into town by river, and a quay was established in Frankwell by Rowland Jenks in 1608. The Shrewsbury Canal was opened in 1797, and brought goods in from the north to its terminus in Howard Street.

During the early nineteenth century, Thomas Telford was engaged to upgrade the London–Holyhead Road. In Frankwell, he reduced the gradient of The Mount by several feet, sinking it below Hermitage Walk, while, in Abbey Foregate, a new section of road to the south of the church was created through the remains of the domestic buildings.

In about 1800, a great deal of new industry developed on the outskirts of town. A woollen mill was erected in Carline Fields in 1790, and was adapted for cotton spinning by Charles Hulbert in 1803. The factory closed in 1814, and was converted into workshops and houses.

In 1795, Thomas and Benjamin Benyon joined John Marshall of Leeds in the flax and linen industry. After a fire burned one of their mills down in Leeds, they rebuilt in Shrewsbury. They were joined by Charles Bage in 1796, and he designed the world's first iron-framed building, which was erected in Ditherington. In 1804, Bage and the Benyons built a second iron-framed mill in Castlefields, and, twelve years later, Bage opened another in Kingsland. This factory was in production for only four years, and was later developed into Burr's Lead Works. The Castlefields mill was closed in 1836 and was largely demolished, except for one building in Severn Street.

The Ditherington factory continued as a textile mill until the end of the century. It was converted, in 1898, into a maltings by William Jones, who had already built two similar businesses in Belle Vue and Castle Foregate. Two large breweries were also set up in the suburbs. The first of these was founded in Chester Street in 1792, by Thomas Hawley. The premises were then acquired by Thomas Southam in 1852. The Old Salop Brewery was founded by Sir John Edenson Heathcote in Coleham in 1805, and purchased by Thomas Trouncer in 1845.

The coming of the railway transformed the face of the landscape dramatically. Many houses were demolished in Howard Street and Castle Hill for the construction of the new station. The communities of Coton Hill and Castle Foregate were severed by the new line and the development of goods yards. Large engine sheds were also built by the different companies in the Coleham area. The Potteries, Shrewsbury & North Wales Railway was opened in 1866, with a station in Abbey Foregate, as the company planned to link The Potteries through Shrewsbury to the Welsh coast, but this never materialized.

By 1851, the population of Shrewsbury had reached over 28,000, making the older suburbs very overcrowded. Many of the ancient burgage plots had been built upon, and families were forced to live in squalid conditions, in small courts whose only access was up narrow alleyways leading off the main road. Vere Place in Castle Foregate was so unhealthy it was known as 'Typhus Square'. During this period, new housing was developed in Castlefields, Ditherington, Belle Vue and Mountfields. In about 1875, Kingsland was developed as a new suburb. Shrewsbury School purchased a large part of the area, which included the House of Industry, and moved there in 1882. The Kingsland Bridge opened the same year, and the corporation was responsible for planning and constructing a new road system over the site, on which superior residences were built. Three other areas were developed on a more modest scale in Cherry Orchard, Copthorne and Greenfields.

During the First World War, great activity was seen around the barracks and elsewhere in the town. This included the opening of a prisoner-of-war camp in Abbey Foregate; a hostel for Belgian refugees in the Armoury, Wenlock Road; a depot in Harlescott for the Royal Flying Corps; an Observer School of Reconnaissance and Aerial Photography at Monkmoor Aerodrome, and, in 1915, Alley & MacLellan of Glasgow established a factory in Harlescott to build steam engines.

Council houses were built in Longden Grove in about 1920, followed later by estates in Judith Butts, Coton Hill and Racecourse Avenue. The Chatwood Safe Company opened a factory in Harlescott in 1928. As was the case with the Sentinel works, a small housing estate provided a good standard of accommodation for the workers. In 1934, the land in Harlescott used by the Royal Flying Corps was developed into a private housing estate by A. & G.P. Fletcher of Blackpool.

During the Second World War, the population of Shrewsbury was swollen by the increase in the number of troops, and The Maltings in Ditherington was converted into a barracks to ease the situation at Copthorne. In 1941, the Shropshire & Montgomery Railway was requisitioned by the War Department to link with the Central Ammunition Storage Depot at Nesscliffe. The old aerodrome at Monkmoor became a recovery and salvage centre for the RAF in 1940 and, in the same year, Vickers Armstrong began to use part of the Midland Red Garage in Ditherington for the production of Spitfire wings. As D-Day approached, the southern end of the new bypass was closed to civilian traffic and filled with military vehicles ready for the Normandy invasion.

The post-war period saw the suburbs develop rapidly. The Sentinel manufactured bathroom and kitchen furniture for use in prefabricated houses, which were being erected in several parts of the town. Large council estates were built at Crowmoor, Springfield and Meole Brace, but by far the biggest area of development was in Harlescott, where the cattle market had moved in 1959.

During the last two decades, much private housing has been developed, building on farmland and absorbing the small hamlets of Sundorne, Sutton, Shelton and Bicton. The town continues to grow, spreading its boundaries even further, creating new suburbs for future generations to study.

This photograph has connections with three of the town's suburbs. It shows the Sentinel Football Club on Frankwell's County Ground. In the background are buildings on Coton Hill. The Sentinel football team were champions of the Shrewsbury & District Works Football League for the 1929/30 season. The cup was presented to them at a social evening held in St Mary's Hall on 22 May 1930. The team members were: F. Lewis, goalkeeper; A. Smith and P. Braddock, fullbacks; J. Glennie, W. Grocott and W. Evans, midfields; and in the forward line, A. Taylor. T. Hodson, W. Braddock, R. Burgess and H. Taylor. Medals were also given to A. Groom and J. Barr. The team dominated the league with a 33-point victory over LMS, the runners up, who achieved 24 points. During the season the Sentinels beat Chatwood 8–0 and Allscott Sugar Beet factory 11–1.

# Section One

# ABBEY FOREGATE
# AND MONKMOOR

*The entrance into Abbey Foregate from the town is over the English Bridge. This*
*photograph shows the bridge before it was widened in 1925. The Congregational church is*
*a handsome Gothic structure, designed by G. Bidlake of Wolverhampton and built by G.*
*Trow & Sons of Wednesbury. It was opened for worship on 31 May 1864, and its first*
*pastor was the Revd Charles Croft. Its spire rises to a height of 115 ft, and it has seating*
*for over 1,000 people. In 1972, when Congregationalists and Presbyterians united, it*
*became a United Reformed church. The building behind the church is the old Shrewsbury*
*National School, erected in 1772.*

The Shrewsbury National School, or Abbey School as it was later known, was originally opened in 1708 on the Wyle Cop side of the English Bridge. Its style of teaching followed a system first introduced by Dr Bell, who inspected the school not long after it was opened. The children dressed in brown, which gave rise to the name 'Brown School'. The children shown on this photograph are, back row, left to right: -?-, Roy France, -?-, -?-, Jack ?, Ron Sturkey, -?-, -?-, Douglas ?. Second row: Joan Knocks, Peggy Dunning. Pauline Hug, Mary Davies, Molly Jones, -?-, Gwen Porter, Marila Phillips, Hilda Pritchard, Barbara Ball. Front row: Maureen Embery, Gwen Bagley, Vera Stubbs, Nora Kings, Nancy Gittins, Kate Davies, -?-, Joyce Wolf, Vera Williams, Ron Catte. The only person to be identified on the front row is the first one on the left, who is Bernard Rock.

Shrewsbury Technical College, *c*. 1930. This house was built by John Carline, a stonemason who came to the town in the eighteenth century to help build the new English Bridge. It became the Borough Technical College in 1899. The college housed technical and commercial classes, a school of art and a centre for training pupil teachers. The building was demolished in 1935.

Abbey Gardens, *c*. 1920. These once belonged to the Carline family and many fragments of their work can still be seen. The park was also known as Mr Palin's Pleasure Gardens, where numerous pieces of ancient architecture were brought and displayed. In the foreground is the Rowley Portal, which has since been returned to the front door of Rowley's Mansion in Hill's Lane.

The two half-timbered houses illustrated on this page stood on either side of the road which now leads down to the Gay Meadow. The house on the left was known as the Old Court House, and it is thought that cases from the Abbey Foregate Great and Small Courts were tried there. The building was demolished in the second half of the nineteenth century. The building below was known as Merivale and was erected in 1601. Unfortunately, it was demolished in 1968, and the site is now used as a car park for the Wakeman School.

The name Merivale applies not only to the house but also to the land that surrounds it. Before the dissolution of The Abbey ownership of the land was often in dispute between the abbot and the bailiffs of Shrewsbury.

This photograph was taken at the Gay Meadow on 12 April 1930, when Shrewsbury Town FC won the Shropshire Senior Cup for the eighteenth time against arch rivals Wellington by three goals to one. A large crowd attended the match and were entertained by some excellent play in the first half. In the second half, both the weather and the play deteriorated. Shrewsbury captain Fred Imbrey was carried off with a lacerated shin, and there was a terrific hail storm, reducing the pitch to a quagmire. Chief Constable Frank Davies presented the cup to Imbrey and the medals to the members of the Shrewsbury team. According to the *Chronicle* the Wellington captain received the runners-up medals in bulk, the other players 'either from modesty or mortification refusing to leave the dressing room'.

The Benedictine Abbey of St Peter and St Paul was founded in 1083 by Roger de Montgomery on the site of a small wooden church dedicated to St Peter. The original church was built during the reign of Edward the Confessor by a Saxon nobleman called Siward. The tower with its fine window, at the western end of the church, was built about 1360, mainly in the Decorated style. The figure above the window represents Edward III, who was king at the time the tower was erected. The statues of St Peter and St Paul with their emblems, the key and the sword, are on either side of the window.

Shrewsbury Abbey, *c*. 1880. After the dissolution of The Abbey in 1540, the whole of the eastern end of the church was destroyed. The west end survived only because it acted as a parish church, with an altar situated in the nave dedicated to the Holy Cross. The eastern window contained six splendid figures in stained glass, the work of local expert David Evans, but was removed when the east end was rebuilt at the end of the nineteenth century. They represented St James, King David, St John and King Solomon in the act of consecrating the temple, and St Peter and St Paul. St Peter still survives in a window in the north aisle.

This photograph was taken outside the west door of The Abbey, in the early 1950s. The shorter of the two clergymen is the vicar, the Revd M.L.A. Wilkinson, who served The Abbey for a quarter of a century until his retirement in 1956. He is with his curate, the Revd Edgar Daniels, and his churchwardens, Mr Barber on the left and Mr Bill Caswell on the right.

During Lent 1958, a Passion play was performed in The Abbey under the direction of the Revd R.J.C. Lumley and the organist and choirmaster, Mr John Stanier. The cast were mainly people from the parish. Back row, left to right: Ted Weaver, Pam Parkes, -?-, Father Barlett (Caiaphas), David Walker, Ralph Stone (Gabriel), Megan Williams, David Brookes (St Peter), Reg Jones, Mrs Morris, Mrs Weston, Mrs Ball and Mrs Bebbington. Second row: Beryl Jones, Raymond Jones (Pilate), Mary Brookes, -?-, Philip Bebbington, -?-, Jonathan Benson, -?-, -?-, -?-, -?-. Front row: first on the left, Hilda Ward; fourth from the right, Gaynor Duffel, who played Mary Magdalene; the others have not been identified.

The refectory pulpit, *c.* 1870. The pulpit stands on its original site, although separated from the church by the main road driven through the old monastic buildings by Thomas Telford in 1835. It is octagonal in shape and was built from Grinshill stone during the latter part of the fourteenth century. At the centre of the domed roof is a boss in the form of a flower, which shows the crucifixion with St John and the Virgin Mary at the foot of the cross. The panels facing the road show the figures of St Peter, St Paul, St Winifred, St Bueno and the Annunciation.

The pulpit used to be used every year on Rogation Sunday. At this service a blessing was asked for the people of the parish, the town and county, and also for their work in industry and agriculture. This photograph was taken at the end of the 1950s, when the vicar, the Revd R.J.C. Lumley, preached the sermon. The last service was held in 1983. In recent years, the pulpit has suffered a great deal of damage through vandalism.

The building housing the Coleham Brush Factory was built in about 1725. The factory was founded in Mardol by William Hudson in 1818. It moved to Coleham in 1889, and to the premises shown here early this century. The Crown has been an inn since 1780 and was once known as the Crow. The Crown has now extended into the brush factory.

This road to the east of The Abbey was once the main route out of town. The house facing us is Abbeydale, built as a private residence early in the eighteenth century. Shrewsbury Technical College was housed there in the 1930s, while the English Bridge site was being rebuilt. The cottages on the right have been replaced with modern town houses.

The fire at Bullock's Timberyard broke out on 6 August 1906 and was fought by the Alliance and Royal Insurance fire brigades. The *Chronicle* reported: 'Burning particles carried by the wind increased the splendour of a magnificent but awesome spectacle. They encircled the stately tower of The Abbey with a fiery mantle which intensified the beauty of the venerable structure, but roused fear for its safety.'

The Shropshire & Montgomeryshire Railway took over The Abbey station around the turn of the century. It was known locally as the 'Slow and Moderate'. During the black-out the driver of a train misjudged the end of the line, ploughed through the buffers, crossed the main road and stopped within inches of The Abbey. Fortunately, no one was injured.

At the rear of these cottages is Cold Bath Court, which refers to a public wash place from the seventeenth and eighteenth centuries. Thomas Howell's book, *A Stranger in Shrewsbury*, makes this short reference to them: 'There are two cold baths, one in Kingsland and the other in the suburb of Abbey Foregate, but neither of them can be recommended as possessing suitable accommodation.'

Abbey Foregate, *c.* 1955. The cottages on the left were demolished towards the end of the 1950s by Safeway's, who developed the town's first supermarket on the site. The house with the handrail was once occupied by Mr W.A. Bilcliff, a professional photographer and verger of The Abbey for many years.

Abbey Foregate, *c.* 1940. The house on the corner of Monkmoor Road was once an inn called the Angel. The property was owned by The Abbey, and was closed down in 1883 after a meeting of the church authorities, who thought it inappropriate that a public house should be run in one of their premises.

The junction of Monkmoor Road and Abbey Foregate, *c.* 1935. This cottage stood on the other corner of Monkmoor Road until the 1960s. It was removed when the road was upgraded to serve the new Telford Way. The house was occupied by Mr George Dickin, a former blacksmith. He kept a herd of cows at the rear and, each morning, would walk them across the Foregate to graze on land on the banks of the Rea Brook.

This photograph was taken at the rear of the Bush Inn, *c.* 1916. The inn was first recorded in about 1700, and was once known as the Hawthorn Bush. The mounted soldier served in the Shropshire Yeomanry. The leather pouch contained a spare horseshoe for emergencies.

Abbey Foregate, *c.* 1940. These cottages, 96–101 Abbey Foregate, were demolished to make way for a block of flats known as Abbey Court. The shop was run by Mrs Emma Mason, who sold groceries and general provisions.

After the building of the Column (see next page), a number of very fine houses were built in the area. This terrace of four houses dates from this period and was erected by John Carline. They have two floors, with a raised attic block over the centre pair. One of The Abbey Trusts still owns two of the houses, which have been turned into flats.

The Woodlands was built at the beginning of the nineteenth century for the Hazeldine family, and it remained a private house until 1930, when it became the Salop Boys Home Police Court Mission. It was converted into a Youth Hostel in 1946.

The Column, *c.* 1890. The first stone of the Column was laid by the Salopian Lodge of Free and Accepted Masons on 27 December 1814, and the last stone on 18 June 1816, the first anniversary of the Battle of Waterloo, at which Lord Hill was one of Wellington's commanders. The overall height of the column is 133 ft 6 in. The statue of Lord Hill, modelled by Panzetta, stands 16 ft high and is made of Coade stone.

The ladies waiting to depart in this marvellous charabanc are members of St Giles' Women's Institute, *c.* 1930. The lady with the feather boa in the centre is Mrs Margaret Spince. They are parked outside the Column Lodge, which used to be occupied by an old soldier who kept the key to the Column. It was demolished when the new Shirehall was built.

St Giles' Church was founded in the twelfth century and formed part of a hospital for lepers. It was part of the parish of the Holy Cross until 1857, when it became a separate parish. Until 1836, it was used mainly for funerals and for worship on two Sunday afternoons in the year. These were known as Eel Pie and Cherry Pie Sundays, and the church was packed for both services. During the second half of the nineteenth century, a great deal of renovation was carried out, thanks to the benevolence of the How family, leaving the church in the fine condition we know today.

The Revd Frederick Roberts became Vicar of St Giles' in 1894. He studied at Trinity College, Dublin, and was curate of Harbourne, Stafford, and St Mary's, Wolverhampton, before moving to Shrewsbury. His stipend, in 1894, was £190 a year. This photograph was taken outside the house of Mr and Mrs Prince on Wenlock Road, by their son, who was a professional photographer.

St Giles' Bible Class, c. 1920. The Bible Class was held at Chaddeslode House by Mrs Owen Evans. Back row, left to right: Lucy Rogers, Bertha Corfield, Marjorie Beaman, -?-. Second row: -?-, Edna Whitefoot, Mrs Owen Evans, Dora Caswell. Front row: Edna Morton, Clarice Turl.

Mill Mead was built as a preparatory school for Shrewsbury and other public schools. The house stands on high ground, with a southern aspect overlooking the hills of south Shropshire and Wales.

Both photographs on this page were taken in about 1920, when the school was under joint headmastership. Both headmasters can be seen in the back row in the photograph above. The shorter man with the cap is Francis Folliot Sandford, who was known to the boys as 'Punch'. The taller man is Arthur Topham Bennion, who stood around 6 ft 3 in.

Whitehall, *c.* 1920. Dr Samuel Butler, Head of Shrewsbury School and Bishop of Lichfield, bought the Whitehall Estate in about 1820. It later passed on to his grandson Samuel, the author, who lived at Clifford's Inn, London. In 1886, a housing estate was planned on land to the north and east of the mansion. Its streets were named by Samuel as Bishop and Canon in memory of his grandfather and father, Clifford after his London home, and Alfred in recognition of his faithful clerk and valet, Alfred Cathie.

The junction of Crowmere Road, Monkmoor Road and Tankerville Street, 3 July 1914. George V, followed by the Shropshire Yeomanry Cavalry, is entering the Racecourse for the Royal Show. This was the seventy-fifth show to be held, and the third to be staged in Shrewsbury, the previous occasions being in 1845 and 1884. The show came to the town again in 1949, when it was held at Sundorne.

The Abbey Parish Hall, *c.* 1953. Eighty children packed the parish hall to celebrate the coronation of Queen Elizabeth II. They were entertained by Mr Dew, a conjuror, and also with a film show. In the centre are the vicar and his wife, Mr and Mrs Wilkinson; the curate on the right is Father Andrews.

Another event to be staged in the parish hall was the annual sale of work, here *c.* 1958. The flowers are being presented by Jane Pyatt. Immediately behind her is her father, Fred Pyatt, who served on the Parochial Church Council for many years as churchwarden and treasurer. Also watching are Preb. Ralph Lumley, Mr Morris and Mr Bill Caswell.

Cherry Orchard Jazz Band, Chester Street. The band was started in about 1930 by Richard Almark, who kept the White Hart in Mardol. It practised in the Tankerville Hall during the winter and in a field in Underdale during the summer. Leading the band is Sonny Weaver; the girl with the banner on the left is Nelly Holmes.

The Ice House, *c.* 1914. According to local legend, this house was the monks' cold store and was connected to The Abbey by an underground passage. Standing outside are the Evans family, who ran a dairy farm from here. On fields stretching up to Judith Butts, they kept a herd of over forty prime dairy cattle.

The Racecourse, *c.* 1890. The course was laid out in 1834 on land known as the Soldier's Piece. Racing ceased in 1887, because of alleged bribery and corruption on the course. At one of the last meetings the horse of a mounted policeman bolted at the start of a race. It was leading into the last bend, but was just pipped at the post!

Several men from Monkmoor made up the 9th Salop (27 GPO) Battalion Shropshire Home Guard. This platoon was one of the best equipped in the Home Guard. Back row, second from the left, Cyril Ford; third from the left, Mr Davies; sixth from the left, Mr Crump. Front row, first on the left, Platoon Sergeant Billy Higgins.

Underdale Ferry, *c.* 1900. The ferry commenced work in November 1882, at the start of Race Week. It was in operation until the Castle Walk footbridge was opened in 1910, which gave easier access from Cherry Orchard to Castlefields. The name Underdale is derived from Hundrethale, a 'hundred' being a division of land and 'hale' a riverside meadow.

St Peter's Church was consecrated by the Bishop of Stafford on 25 March 1939. The church was packed, and quite a number of people were unable to get in. Some members of The Abbey Choir were late and were seen running up Monkmoor Road, one dropping his ruffle in the mud.

Part of Monkmoor Hospital was built in 1918 as a women's hostel connected with the airfield. At this time, Monkmoor Hall was the town's isolation hospital, along with a smallpox unit in Underdale Road. The hostel was converted, in 1921, by the Shrewsbury and Atcham Joint Hospital Board and turned into the area's isolation hospital, giving accommodation of about fifty beds. It became a children's hospital in the 1950s, and later, a geriatric unit. The hospital closed in 1991 and was demolished in 1994. The gentleman are being entertained by Matron Ellis.

# Monkmoor Covered Tennis Court
## SHREWSBURY.

### SUMMER AND WINTER.
The 1922 Inter-County Hard Court Championships
WARWICKSHIRE *.* SHROPSHIRE, Ladies Doubles.
CHESHIRE *.* SHROPSHIRE, Gent's Doubles.
Were played on these Courts.

This is one of the Belfast Trussed Hangars built at the top of Monkmoor in the final months of the First World War. The new airfield was used as an Aircraft Acceptance Park and as an Observer School of Reconnaissance and Aerial Photography. This advertisement was taken from a 1922 *Wilding's Directory*, and shows that one of the hangars was used as covered tennis courts. The other was utilized by a poultryman, who set up his hen house in the building. During the Second World War, the RAF used the airfield as a salvage centre. No. 34 Salvage Centre was formed on 1 March 1940. About a dozen teams worked independently under an NCO, recovering crashed or damaged machines from Shropshire, the surrounding counties and North Wales. The hangar is now divided into three units on the Monkmoor Trading Estate.

# Section Two

# COLEHAM AND BELLE VUE

*The English Bridge replaced the Old Stone Bridge and was erected between 1769 and 1774. In the background is Carline Fields, a group of small houses built on land named after the family of stonemasons. Sitting on the confluence of the Rea Brook and the Severn, they were liable to flooding. When the new houses were built on this site, the land was raised by several feet.*

Coleham Head, *c.* 1920. References to the Swan Inn have been made since 1650. By the 1920s, it was owned by F.W. Soames & Co. The landlord, Arthur Causer, can be seen at the door. He was a professional footballer, playing in goal for both Preston Northend and Shrewsbury. The inn was de-licensed on 30 June 1928, and demolished soon afterwards. It was replaced by a pair of shops which stand on the traffic island caused by the building of the new gyratory system.

Coleham, *c.* 1958. The white building is the Seven Stars public house. There were two inns of that name in Coleham, standing very close to one another. Both were there in 1786, but one had gone by 1820. To the left of the Seven Stars is the Black Horse, first recorded in 1874. This hostelry was always popular with the men who worked on the old Great Western Railway.

Strefford's Garage, also known as Carline Motor Works, *c.* 1920. He guaranteed first-class repairs with the finest engineering plant in the district. The sign in the top right-hand corner reminds us that Mr Cooper, who kept a large fleet of pleasure boats under the Kingsland Bridge, also had a workshop on the Rea Brook.

Until the building of Moreton Crescent in the middle of the nineteenth century, Old Coleham was the main road out of Shrewsbury to Meole Brace and Bayston Hill. The building on the right-hand corner was the home of W.R. Pugh, the undertaker. It was demolished in December 1978.

This is a rare photograph of Old Coleham during the floods of 1946. The cottages were demolished a number of years ago. The building on the right, with the double doors, has been used as a blacksmith's forge and a garage.

The Abbey Works, *c*. 1920. These works, once owned by railway contractor R.S. Francis, lay between Coleham and Abbey Foregate. In 1877 it was bought by the Midland Wagon Co. Ltd. During the First World War, the buildings were adapted into a prisoner-of-war camp. The area has recently been redeveloped by Safeway's supermarket.

Midland Carriage and Wagon Works, *c.* 1890. Shortly after taking over the factory in 1877, the company changed its name to the Midland Railway Carriage and Wagon Co. Ltd. The works was one of the largest employers in the town, giving employment to several hundred men. Between 1877 and 1912, this was the company's main factory, making the majority of all the firm's passenger vehicles. The works closed  vhen a new factory was built at Washwood Heath, Birmingham.

Rocke Street, *c.* 1916. This unique photograph was taken during the First World War and was published by the Red Cross in Geneva for sale in Germany. The caption on the card reads 'Marching out a German work column'. The Germans were from the prisoner-of-war camp situated in the old Midland Carriage Works and are marching up Rocke Street. The cottages on the left still exist, but the old locomotive sheds at the end of the street have been demolished. The street was named after the Rocke family of Sutton, who owned land here in 1655. The cottages here and in adjacent streets housed many railway workers, and were known locally as 'Back of the Sheds'.

The Sheds, *c.* 1950. The engine on the turntable is a Great Western 'Manor'. The turntable could be operated manually by one man, or automatically when coupled up to the engine's vacuum-brake system, if the engine had enough steam. The buildings at the rear are the old LMS engine sheds.

Holy Trinity Church, *c.* 1910. This was erected as a chapel of ease in the suburb of Belle Vue in 1837. It formed a new parish out of St Julian's in 1840. The building has had many additional features built on. In 1847 a new vestry was built, in 1861 a new chancel was added, and finally, in 1885, a nave and aisles were erected.

The first children's crossing was opened on 1 February 1948. The children are from Coleham School, and are crossing from the bottom of Trinity Street. The opening was carried out by Mr Perks, a local councillor, under the watchful eye of PC Othen. By November 1949, another five crossings were operating in the town.

Coleham Girls Athletic Team won the Elementary School Sports Shield for the third time in June 1930. This was the ninth annual sports, and it was held on the Gay Meadow. The mayor, Mr Woolham, presented the shield to Coleham, who scored thirty points. The results for the girls' team were: 100 yards, K. Corfield 1st, N. Phillips 3rd; 80 yards, W. Barre 1st; 100 yards skipping, N. Phillips 1st, M. Martin 2nd; obstacle race, M. Lowe 2nd; standing long jump, N. Peplow 1st with 8 ft 1 in, a new record; netball shooting, M. Lloyd 2nd; relay, Coleham girls 1st.

The Limes, *c.* 1900. The house was built by Samuel Pountney-Smith, who was mayor in 1873. He also built Oakley Manor in Belle Vue, shown in the picture below. The Limes became a school towards the end of the nineteenth century. Mr Drew, the headmaster, took boys from the ages of seven to fourteen and prepared them for scholarship and entrance examinations for Shrewsbury and other public schools.

From the outbreak of the First World War until March 1917, Oakley Manor was adapted into a St John's Auxiliary Military Hospital. Several hundred men were treated here, and their recoveries were greatly aided by the pleasant surroundings. In 1916, the house was purchased by Mr Della Porta, the owner of a large store in town. Another well-known businessman, Arthur Vincent Greenhous, bought the property in 1929 as a family home. In May 1962, the house was purchased by Shrewsbury Borough Council.

Coleham, *c*. 1946. The older people of Coleham remember with affection the bread and cakes baked at the shop of John Cock, behind the people in the punt. The chip shop on the corner of Longden, Coleham and Moreton Crescent was once known as 'Cocoa House', a temperance alternative to the public house as a place to sit and talk.

Coleham was heavily industrialized in the nineteenth century, and rows of small cottages were built to house the workforce. The houses on the left were demolished in the 1970s. The area has always been greatly affected by floods, as the picture above demonstrates. The Seven Stars once had a plaque over the mantelpiece stating: 'To our very great surprise the Severn to this place did rise.'

This site above School Lane was redeveloped in the 1970s. The shop on the corner was Richard Meyrick's fried fish shop. The house in the centre was a barber's shop run by John Boylin. It was also a second-hand shop. The next house was recorded from 1851 as the Three Tuns, until its licence was transferred to the Pengwern Hotel in 1938. It was an alehouse belonging to Trouncers, the local brewery. The inn also gave its name to the passage on the right.

This VE-day party, held in School Lane, was organized by the Salvation Army and by Mrs Hands, the landlady of the Hen and Chickens. The Coleham Jazz Band paraded the streets throughout the day and played outside the inn for dancing.

This photograph of Lowcock's Foundry was taken in August 1934, not long before the buildings were demolished. The factory was established by William Hazeldine, who worked closely with Thomas Telford on a number of projects, including the building of the Menai Bridge. The ironwork used on the bridge was cast and proved here by an engine whose test pressure was calculated at 37 tons. Hazeldine's first foundry in Shrewsbury was at Coleshall, in Barker Street. The works were sold to Arthur Lowcock, who made the famous Lowcock Fuel Economiser for heating the water to steam boilers, using 20 per cent less coal.

Coleham, *c.* 1934. Mrs Allen's shop occupied part of Lowcock's Foundry on the corner of the entrance to Greyfriars Bridge. Mrs Allen sold all types of second-hand furniture. The Greyfriars Bridge was opened in 1880, replacing a ferry owned by William Trouncer.

Trouncer's Brewery, *c.* 1895. The drayman is Thomas Williams, who was employed by Trouncer's. On 22 May 1899, while returning to the brewery with a dray full of empty barrels, his horse was startled by a car. Mr Williams tried to jump from the dray, but two wheels passed over him. He died later in the Salop Infirmary.

## Section Three

# KINGSLAND

*The Prince of Wales, c. 1880. The life of this inn was very short, as it existed for only a few years towards the end of the nineteenth century. The building was then used as the residence of the boatman for Shrewsbury School. Evans' Boat House to the left was used by Pengwern Boat Club and the Schools to store their boats. When Pengwern moved to their new club house in 1881, the Schools took over the site and built their own boat-house.*

This photograph of Kingsland, *c.* 1930, shows Shrewsbury School, complete with all its buildings, fifty years after it left its town site. The main building was erected as a foundling hospital by Thomas Coram in about 1760. The hospital closed in 1772 and, a few years later, was converted into a gaol for Dutch prisoners of war. The Union of Parishes bought the property in 1784, as a workhouse. The workhouse closed in 1875, and, in 1879, work began to develop the area. Shrewsbury School officially moved on to this site in the summer of 1882.

The fire which engulfed Shrewsbury School on 5 December 1905 was discovered a few minutes before noon. One of the boys, hearing a crackling noise, looked up and saw sparks coming from a ventilator on the roof. The alarm was raised but, within the hour, the whole top floor was ablaze.

Two ladders joined together were used to reach the roof but, with the weight of three men and two hoses, it broke. Alfred Jones and Sam Plimmer were hurled to the ground, while the ladder fell among the spectators, scattering them in all directions. Plimmer was only slightly hurt, but Jones was kept in the infirmary.

The Prince of Wales visited Shrewsbury School on 21 June 1932. Accompanied by Canon Sawyer, the Earl of Powis, Viscount Bridgeman and the mayor, he moved over to the site of the new foundation for the old school wall. Lord Bridgeman explained how the wall had been brought from the old school and contained the names of former athletes carved into the stone. Before laying the foundation stone, HRH received a mounted silver trowel from the architect, Mr J.A. Forsyth, and a mounted silver mallet from the builder, Mr T. Morris.

The Fives Courts, c. 1910. When the game of fives was first played at Shrewsbury is unknown but, at the old school, it was played with a 21-inch bat on two courts below the main school building. These courts were built soon after the move from town, when the use of the bat was dropped and the Eton game of hand-fives was adopted.

Chessington and Beech Hill, *c.* 1910. These houses were built on Kennedy Road by H. Treasure, a well-known builder in the town. He built a number of other houses in Kingsland; bricks were supplied from his brickworks in Woodfield and taken to the site on a narrow-gauge railway. The first occupants of the houses were William Thorne and Mrs Sarah Jenkins. This photograph was taken after the building had been extensively altered. The principal roads in the area are all named after former headmasters of Shrewsbury School: Samuel Butler, Thomas Ashton and Benjamin Hall Kennedy.

Cyngfeld, *c.* 1920. This is the largest and grandest of the houses built on Kingsland in the nineteenth century. It was the home of E. Cresswell Peele, a local solicitor, clerk of the county and also town clerk. He had an interest in so many things in the county that he was nicknamed 'The Lord High Everything Else'.

Kingsland Grange School, *c.* 1920. Early in the twentieth century, the school was run by Mr W.B.C. Drew, BA, who was headmaster at the Limes School. Boarders enjoyed all possible home comforts under the special care of Mrs Drew. Pupils were prepared for entrance to public schools and the Royal Naval College at Osborne.

# FRANKWELL AND COPTHORNE

*The towpath which runs along the Frankwell side of the river is known as Silk's Meadow
Walk. In 1360, it belonged to William Selk, but later the land passed to the Mytton
family and formed part of their large estate. At the close of the nineteenth century, it
belonged to Richard Bromley, a local councillor and businessman, who donated part of it
as a recreation area for the people of Frankwell. Frankwell is often referred to as the 'Little
Boro', because of its origins and strong independent nature.*

Frankwell, *c.* 1900. This is the first of the many timber-framed buildings we see in Frankwell as we cross the Welsh Bridge. The extensive frontage rising up three storeys was originally built as one house. In the last century, part of the building was an inn known as the Fox. It was skilfully renovated by Mr Eldred, one of the proprietors of Eldred, Mottram & Co., who had a shop there.

This house was known, in the nineteenth century, as the Sweep's Lodging House and was run by the Evans family for many years. Their main guests were usually hawkers and street peddlars, but occasionally a touring German band was recorded as staying there. During the twentieth century, it was the home of Tommy Davies, another local sweep. Mrs Davies used to make toffee apples, which she sold for 1*d* each. Her shop was described in the old *Frankwell Observer* as the 'House of the Big Apple'. The house was demolished in the 1960s, and the space is used as a car park for a local auctioneer's business.

This photograph records Frankwell Quay as it was sixty years ago. The quay was opened in 1608, and river traffic from as far upstream as Pool Quay and downstream to Bristol docked and traded here. Along this short frontage, four of the buildings have at some time in their history been public houses. The first house on the left was the Speed and Plough, or just the Plough. The timber-framed building was once the Dog and Badger. At the far end of the row is the Anchor, which still survives, and next to that, the large building that juts out on the corner is the White Horse, which gave its name to the passage leading into Mountfields. As if to try and counter the evils of drink, a Mr Forrest set up his mission room in the house to the right of the timber-framed building.

Frankwell always maintained its right to hold its own carnival, and huge crowds used to pack the quay to see the fun. A large banner went over the Welsh Bridge, proclaiming: 'Out of the Land of Sin' [Shrewsbury] 'Into the Land of Purity' [Frankwell]. People passing over the bridge were charged 1*d*.

First to appear on the quay was the 'Royal Coach', having travelled down Frankwell from the Buck's Head. It was guarded by 'foot soldiers' and 'cavalry'. 'King Gudgeon' was Wallace Steventon, and his 'Queen' was local barber Natty Price. The coach driver was Mr Ernie Welsby. Both of these photographs depict the carnival of 1936.

In September 1938, the mayor of Frankwell, Wallace Steventon, welcomed the mayor of Shrewsbury, Alderman Beddard, and his daughter, to the Frankwell Carnival for the opening of the Treasure Chest. A joyful shout went up when a large barrel of beer was found. The 'lady in waiting' is Mr Charles Morley, landlord of the Cross Guns.

'King Farouk's Court'. Frankwell Carnival, 1952. The 'harem', left to right: Jim Foley, Bert Chant, Albert Millington, Cyril Hunt, Will Lock. The royal couple are represented by Tom Cartwright as the 'Queen' and Ron Price as King Farouk. The 'constables' are (left) Buster Jones and (right) Jack Thorpe.

This photograph was taken in 1958, just before the demolition of the small cottages. It shows two of Frankwell's greatest characters, Ernie Welsby on the left and Natty Price. Mr Welsby was a general dealer in the area for many years, carrying out his business from a yard at the bottom of Water Lane. He was, on many occasions, the Mayor of Frankwell. Natty Price ran a barber's shop in the first cottage on the left for nearly half a century. It was the local gossip shop, the *Frankwell Observer* saying that 'he [Natty] is the greatest living exponent of the talking machine, flying from one topic to another with the greatest of ease'. This part of Frankwell is still known as 'Natty Price's Corner'.

Natty Price's Corner, *c.* 1960. The timber-framed building was demolished overnight after lying derelict for a number of years. The Wheatsheaf, a public house since 1856, had the brick frontage removed. The new flats behind the scaffolding were built above the flood line by local builder Frank Galliers.

Topping-out ceremony, Natty Price's Corner, *c.* 1960. Standing, left to right: -?-, -?-, Jack Powis, Ceddy Bunce, ? Powis, Eddy Purslow, -?-, Charley Powis. Kneeling: Ossey Oakley, Bill Golby.

Frankwell, *c.* 1910. In recent years, a great deal of restoration has been carried out in the Frankwell area. During the 1950s, there were rumours of the wholesale destruction of the buildings on the right. The building with the tall gable on the right used to house the Bell Inn. There was a dance hall at the rear, frequented by the locals and soldiers from the barracks.

Frankwell, *c.* 1900. The junction of Frankwell and New Street was widened at the turn of the century, when the Home and Colonial was demolished and the corner widened. The String of Horses became a public house in about 1804. It has also been known as the Royal Oak and the Cross Keys.

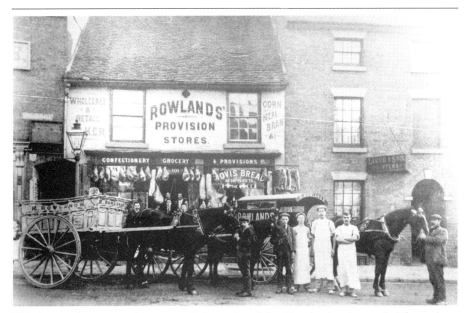

This impressive array of transport belonged to John Rowland, who traded from these premises between 1896 and 1903. The firm still trades in the town from the Old Brewery in Coleham. These premises are now occupied by Abbeycolor. To the right is the Little Boro's own printer, Abraham Lloyd. Until the 1950s local traders could supply most of the needs of the local population.

Frankwell, c. 1940. The building on the left was the home of Edward Owen, a local water diviner and well digger. He was known locally as 'Neddy Pump'. The house, which was reputed to have the highest gable in Shrewsbury, was demolished with the building of the Frankwell roundabout.

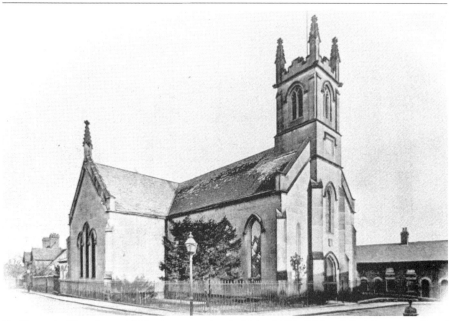

St George's Church, *c.* 1930. At a meeting held in 1827, Richard Drinkwater offered this land for the erection of St George's as a chapel of ease connected to St Chad's. The church was consecrated in 1832, and was formed into a separate parish in 1837. It commemorates the medieval chapel of St George, which stood near the old Welsh (or St George's) Bridge.

'Hermitage Walk', *c.* 1935. The name refers to a hermit who lived near Cadogan's Cross on The Mount. The cottages, which date from about 1800, are thought to have housed the gardeners who worked for Dr Robert Darwin at Darwin House. The cottage behind the lamp post had a beautiful sundial at the rear.

St George's FC, *c*. 1923/4. In the last quarter of the nineteenth century, there were three football clubs in Frankwell. They were the Millington's Club, the Cottage Club and the Frankwell Club. St George's Church formed a club after 1918. *Eddowes Press* reported a match between Millington's and St Chad's, played on the Racecourse. The game was carried on with great spirit for about two hours. The result was a 2–0 victory for Millington's. This photograph, taken outside the Millington's Hospital, shows, back row, left to right: Sam ?, Frank Page, Ern Kelsall, Albert Page, ? Embrey, ? Francis, -?-, Mr Davies. Second row: George Hall, Mr Harrison, Fred Reece, Art Davies, ? Chelmark, -?-, the Revd Mr Agnew, Edward Hall. Front row: Bill Haycock, Phil Abley, Dick Richards, Harry Galliers, Tommy 'Chipper' Cartwright.

This is the Eldred family outside their home, Court House in Mountfields, *c.* 1918. The pillars to the front door are thought to have come from a house at the top of Mardol, demolished in about 1866. The business of Eldred, Mottram & Co. was founded in 1790.

Darwin House, *c.* 1930. Formerly known as the Mount House, it was built in about 1800 by Dr Darwin, father of Charles Darwin, who was born there in about 1809. In about 1900 it was known as Monkmoor House, that being the name of the former home in Monkmoor Road of the occupier, Col. Phillips. The name 'Darwin House' was in use by 1928.

This police box was placed on The Mount, almost opposite the junction with Hafren Road. It was one of four boxes situated on the outskirts of town and was a valuable means of communication with the police station. In each box there was a small door which, when opened, established a telephone link with the police station. On top of the box was a lamp which could be illuminated from the station in order to get in touch with a police constable on that beat. Each box contained a larger compartment which held a stretcher, a first aid box and a telephone. PC 'Smiler' Stone and Sergeant Edwards are seen visiting the box, which came into operation in July 1931.

The Beauchamp Hotel was built as a private residence on The Mount towards the end of the nineteenth century. It became a hotel in the 1930s, when the proprietress was Mrs Manford. The hotel, set in lovely gardens overlooking the river, was demolished in 1995. Full board in 1938 cost between 2½ and 3½ guineas per week.

The Buck's Head has been a public house since the middle of the nineteenth century. In 1851, the landlord, James Birch, was also one of the local blacksmiths, plying his trade in the yard at the rear. The cottages next to the inn were demolished in the early 1970s.

All these cottages were demolished to make way for Frankwell traffic island. The first cottage on the right was once a small provisions shop run by Thomas Grain. For a very short period during the nineteenth century, the house above the timber-framed cottages was an inn known as the Golden Lion.

Chapel Street was a short road linking Frankwell and New Street. It contained lots of narrow courts, full of small cottages. The building behind the van housed St George's Infant School, founded in 1829 by Dr Darwin. In the early years, the school was run by his daughters, Susan and Emily. The building was demolished in 1994.

This photograph was taken in about 1880, from the top of Millington's Hospital. St George's Boys School was built on the lower section of land to the right of the path, and behind that, St George's Parish Hall. The gymnastic equipment was used by the pupils attending Millington's School.

Millington's Hospital, *c.* 1880. James Millington died in February 1739 and, in his will, he left the bulk of his wealth for the foundation of a hospital to be named after him. The hospital was built as a home for the old and a school for the poor, and was ready for occupation in August 1749. This photograph shows some of the residents outside their cottages in the last quarter of the nineteenth century. The gentleman wearing the mortar board is schoolmaster Mr William Harrison, who was in charge of the school from 1879 to 1891. While at the school, Mr Harrison's youngest son was left paralysed after falling 20 ft from the terrace wall.

St George's Parish Hall, *c.* 1960. The hall was an old army hut purchased by the Revd A.T. Agnew (see page 70) after the First World War and erected on Millington's land. The hall was taken down in October 1977. Over the years, many functions have been held there, including the VE-day party below, held on 23 May 1945.

Many residents in Frankwell worked hard to provide a marvellous tea, which was followed by ice-cream and games. Each child was then presented with an orange and a shilling. Left aisle, third from front: Mrs L. Corfield. Middle aisle, first from front: Mrs Jones, third from front: Mrs Burson. Right aisle, first from front: Mrs Wallace, third from front: Mrs Blakemore and fourth from front: Mrs Richards.

The Revd A.T. Agnew cuts the cake at the St George's Darby and Joan Club Christmas party, 1952. This scholarly Scotsman became vicar in 1923 and served the parish until his death in a road accident in 1961. Always a popular man, this verse was written about him in the *Chronicle* in 1939. 'Though he hails from Bonnie Scotland/ He dwells amongst the Franks,/ That gay and proud community who dwell on Severn's banks;/ Claiming status as a borough, and if their claim be true/ Our subject who is vicar must rank as Chaplain too./ He's a worker for the Legion, he did his bit in France/ And has a gift for writing plays with merry song and dance./ He wrote a play about the Mayor of Frankwell, and they say/ That all the things he prophesied will come to pass one day.' Photographed with the vicar, back row left, first three: Mrs Bradley, Miss Davies, Mrs Buckley; front row, first left: Mr Cookson, third left: Mrs MacNamara.

New Street, *c.* 1890. The name first arose in about 1700. Before this, it was known as Slah Street or Norton's Lane. The shop next to Rowlands was a bakery belonging to Mr Edwards. Prior to this, the premises were used as a public house, recorded first as the Crow, and later the New Inn. It was the last inn in Shrewsbury to retain a mounting block at the front door.

This photograph shows the Queen and her entourage travelling down New Street after her visit to Kingsland on 24 October 1952. Before visiting Shrewsbury School, the Queen had lunched at the castle with the mayor and inspected a guard of honour of young cadets.

Bugle Major Ted Potts leading the band of the 4th Battalion King's Shropshire Light Infantry up New Street. The band are wearing scarlet tunics, one of the last units in the British Army to do so. The building advertising Wilderspools Ales is the Cross Guns.

Mrs Gibbons ran this grocery shop in New Street for many years. Before that, it was owned by Mrs Cooper, whose sons helped found the auctioneering business of Cooper and Green. The shop was in front of the present post office. Walking past is Mr Ackers, a local painter and decorator. This photograph dates from about 1959.

New Street, *c.* 1958. The section of road from the bottom of Copthorne to Porthill was once known as Boathouse Lane. Five houses from Mrs Gibbon's shop on the left is another shop belonging to Bert Harris. The house on the right was once the home of Mr Charlie Wilding, a well-known local athlete.

A great deal of demolition took place in New Street in about 1959–60. The buildings being knocked down are part of Maddox Buildings. They were built in about 1830 by John Maddox, a local maltster who lived at Quarry View House. Watching the work is Mr Tom Corfield, on the right.

This photograph of the bottom of New Street was taken from Pritchard's Nursery, *c.* 1890. The cottages in the foreground were built at the beginning of the nineteenth century. The one on the left nearest Water Lane was an inn called the Alma. Severn Lodge (right foreground) was built in the Gothic style and was the home of Revd J.H. Charter, a member of Shrewsbury School's board.

Sandhurst was built in the early twentieth century for Samuel Withers on land belonging to Pritchard's Nursery. Mr Withers was the proprietor of The Motor House, one of the town's largest garages, on Mardol Quay. He was also a local councillor representing the Quarry Ward.

The photographs on this page show both sides of the Boat House, a timber-framed building at the foot of Porthill. In the seventeenth century, the inn belonged to the Harwood family, who also owned The Ship in Bridge Street and several barges and trows on the river.

The manually operated ferry took passengers across the river for $\frac{1}{2}d$. The rope could be lowered into the water to allow larger boats to pass. The ferry, which had been used for over two hundred years, stopped when the new Porthill Bridge was opened in 1922.

The Frankwell Musical Nuts, *c.* 1914. This group of men raised money for many causes by providing moments of melody and madness. The drummer is Harry Pugh. On his right are Alf Gill and Charles Davies. On his left is George Sandford, and just behind him, F.S. Jones. The man in the helmet is Grove Hall. Towards the top left, with the heavy, black beard, is Natty Price.

Copthorne, *c.* 1958. The name probably derives from the 'cop' or hill top with thorn trees, and is mentioned as early as 1605. The man in the white coat is Mr Freddy Green, standing outside his garage. On the right is St George's Boys' School, demolished in 1994.

The pupils of St George's Girls' School, c. 1900. They pose proudly in their Union Jack dresses made especially for Empire Day. Early in the twentieth century, Empire Day celebrations took place either on the Racecourse in Monkmoor or by the bandstand in The Quarry. All the schools would assemble there and, after being addressed by the mayor, the children would sing several patriotic songs. They would then march back to their school before being dismissed for a half day's holiday.

St George's Boys Football Team, 1938/9. St George's has always produced good sportsmen, especially in football and swimming. This photograph was taken on the County Ground. Back row, left to right: Charles Haddock, -?-, Reg Clements, Eric Page, -?-, Les Griffiths, George Bailey. Front row: John Buttry, ? Davies, Trevor Passant, Arthur Mansell, Charles Price.

Copthorne Barracks, c. 1895. These are regular KSLI soldiers. They are wearing scarlet tunics with blue collar and cuffs, blue trousers with narrow red stripe, and white leather equipment. Their headgear was either the blue spiked helmet or the black Glengarry cap.

Mytton Oak Road, c. 1935. The road was named in 1934, after Mytton Oak House. Oakfield Road is to the right of the car. Since this photograph was taken, the road has been widened, the telegraph poles have disappeared and road traffic has increased dramatically!

Woodfield, *c.* 1910. This unique photograph shows Brooklyn Cottage and the site of the former brickworks belonging to Mr Treasure, the builder. In the late nineteenth century bricks made here were taken by narrow-gauge railway to the building site on Kingsland. This shot shows, from the left, Jack Kelsall, who owned the property, looking towards the line of horses. The first is an 18 ft timber carriage pulled by Charlie and a half-legged chain horse called Tommy, with waggoner Tommy Vaughan at their head. Sitting on the timber, which was sold for decorative purposes, is Ern Kelsall. The next cart was pulled by Dragon, with waggoner Harry Jones and young Bill Kelsall leaning over the side. Next in line is Bill Lewis, with Captain, the horse with the white feet. Other waggoners include Jack Frost, who was also a local preacher, and Tom Lewis, Bill's brother.

# CHESTER STREET
# TO COTON HILL

*Chester Street, c. 1930. Chester Street was once known as Bagley Bridge. The bridge used to carry the main road out of town over the Bagley Brook. The public house was first recorded as the Greyhound in 1879, in memory of Master McGrath, three times winner of the Waterloo Cup. The hound, owned by Lord Lurgan, was so famous it was received at Court by Queen Victoria. All the buildings on the left were demolished in 1939 to widen the approach to Chester Street and the entrance to Smithfield Road.*

The junction of Smithfield Road and Chester Street, *c.* 1890. This business was founded by J.G. Spence in 1820, and was acquired by William Howe in 1883. The shop, which sold a wide range of ironmongery, furniture and farm equipment, was ideally situated between the cattle market and the railway station.

Chester Street, *c.* 1930. Like most of the town's suburbs, Chester Street is prone to flooding. The grocery business on the left was run for many years by Mrs Mary Morris. The vehicle is parked outside Southam's Brewery.

Benbow House, Coton Hill, *c.* 1920. The house was the birthplace of Admiral Benbow, the 'Nelson' of the seventeenth century. For a number of years in the nineteenth century, it was used as St Mary's Vicarage. In about 1910, Mark Davies, the proprietor of a garage on Dogpole, opened another branch in the garden of this house.

Mark Davies's garage was bought, in 1919, by Cyril Harrison-Watson, who had founded Furrows a year earlier. There has never been a Mr Furrow. The name comes from the furrows ploughed up by tractors used by Mr Harrison-Watson for a government food production scheme during the First World War.

Centuries ago, the Severn formed a large, northerly loop reaching to Hencott and entering the present river at Bagley Bridge. The area it contained was known as the Isle of Coton. This road has also been known as the Wem Road.

The large, timber-framed building was once the great barn belonging to the Mytton family, who built a mansion here in about 1500. During the nineteenth century, an undertaker used to display his coffins leaning on the wall. On the right is the shop of George King, official barber in Coton Hill for over fifty years.

The Bird In Hand, Coton Hill, *c.* 1926. This public house was first recorded in 1780. It is thought that the name comes from the old proverb, 'a bird in the hand is worth two in the bush', and usually meant that no credit would be given. Standing on the steps are the landlord, Mr Richard Evans, and his son, Victor.

Coton Hill and Frankwell were once joined together. The Popsey Island on the right was the site of a musical and floral fête. A bridge of barges and planks was laid across the river for public access. During the evening of the 1878 show, a sudden shower sent a crowd scurrying for the bridge. It collapsed, throwing over a hundred people into the Severn. In the confusion, ten people drowned.

This photograph shows the remains of Coton Hill (North) signal box, which was completely destroyed by fire in October 1955. There was no ready water supply for the fire brigade to fight the fire, and 200 ft of hose was used to get water from a hydrant in Coton Crescent. The alarm was raised by signalman Ron Brooks, who had just started his night shift in the box. The Paddington–Birkenhead express was held up for twenty minutes at Shrewsbury, and freight trains were delayed by several hours.

# CASTLE FOREGATE

# AND CASTLEFIELDS

*This unusual view was taken in Castle Foregate in 1892. It can be dated so accurately*

*from one of the posters on the corner of Cross Street. The railway bridge was built in*

*1848 to carry the Shrewsbury–Chester line. In about 1900, it was altered and extended*

*several yards up the Foregate. On the left are two public houses, the Old House at Home in*

*the timber-framed building, and the Eagle on the corner of Howard Street.*

This view was taken from Howard Street, *c.* 1895. On the left is Cross Street. The shop on the corner was run by Henry Done, a grocer. He was also a tea blender and baker. Two doors away is Coal Wharf Tavern, and another inn, the Traveller's Rest, is towards the end of the row.

Wharf Road, *c.* 1890. The road celebrates the opening of the Shrewsbury Canal in 1796. The ironmongers was owned by J.G. Spence, who also had a large warehouse and implements depot further up the road. The business was bought by Richard Chidley in 1886. The site is now occupied by the Royal Mail sorting office.

Corbett's Perseverance Ironworks was completely destroyed during the early hours of 20 November 1905. The blaze was fought by the town's two insurance fire brigades, and damage was estimated at more than £8,000. Morris's Oilworks now occupies the site, which was the scene of another disastrous fire in 1954.

Walker's Bakery, *c.* 1900. It opened in these premises in about 1898. It was described as the most complete bakery in the Midlands, and personal visits were invited. They also sold home-cured hams and bacon, and their vans delivered to all parts of the town. Morris's took them over in 1918.

The Gas Works, c. 1960. Shrewsbury Gas Light Company was formed in 1820. The building being demolished is the carbonizing plant, which was brought into operation in June 1932. The Woodhall-Duckham Continuous Vertical Retorts were capable of carbonizing 80.4 tons of coal and producing 1,460,000 cubic ft of gas a day.

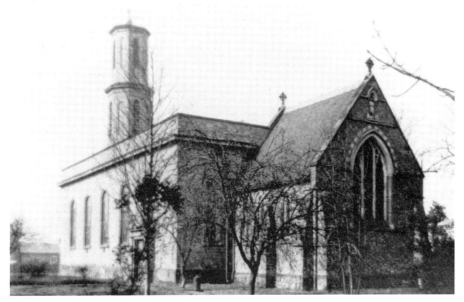

St Michael's Church, c. 1930. There was a medieval chapel dedicated to St Michael in Shrewsbury Castle, whose parish reached into the northern suburb of Castle Foregate. In 1829, this land was bought by the parisoners of St Mary's for a church and cemetery.

The new church was consecrated on 24 August 1830, and was dedicated to St Michael. It was built in the Grecian style, with an unusual octagonal tower. The architect was John Carline, and it was built for around £2,000. When the church became redundant, it was bought by the freemasons. The vicar here is the Revd Mr Holmes.

St Michael's Gardens, c. 1970. This terrace of twelve houses was built some time between 1830 and 1850. They were bought in 1926 by William Jones, who owned the Maltings, but were sold ten years later. Another group of houses, known as 'Davies's Buildings', once stood to the right of the terrace.

St Michael's Gardens VE-day party. Back row, left to right: Elwyn Davies, Christine Jago, June Powell, Fred Davies, Christopher and Mrs Dean. Second row: David Powell, David Croft, Margaret Jago, Michael Powell, Terry Croft. Front row: Raymond Harris, Pearl Davies, Elaine Davies, Geoffrey Croft, Sheila Harris. Mrs Dean kept the post office on St Michael's Street.

The Maltings, *c.* 1950. This large building was built as a flax mill by John Marshall and Thomas and Benjamin Benyon in 1796–7. It was the first building to have a frame completely constructed from iron. It was designed by Charles Bage and is the prototype of the modern skyscraper. The iron used was cast at William Hazeldine's foundry in Coleham. In 1897, William Jones converted the buildings into maltings. During the Second World War, they were used as a barracks, but in 1945 reverted to their former use until 1987, when they were closed. Note the dry bed of the Shrewsbury Canal on the right.

The Midland Red Garage, *c.* 1925. The Allen Omnibus Co. Ltd of London, who had maintained an outpost in Shrewsbury, was taken over by the Midland Red on 1 April 1916. This garage was built on the site of the Sultan Inn in about 1920. The man on the far left is Harry Broadhurst.

During the Second World War, the right-hand section of the garage was adapted into No. 5 Factory, making Spitfire wings needed at Cosford. A small number of experienced fitters were transferred from Castle Bromwich, but the majority of the workforce, mainly women and totalling four hundred, was recruited locally.

Howard Street, *c.* 1895. This street takes its name from John Howard, the famous eighteenth-century reformer, whose bust can be seen over the main gateway into Shrewsbury Prison. The gaol was constructed between 1787 and 1793. The warehouse half-way up the bank was opened as a butter and cheese market at the terminus of the Shrewsbury Canal in 1835. The building on the corner was the Eagle Hotel. From 1860, it was used by carriers to Hodnet. It was also popular with cyclists and travelling salesmen. Since the realignment of the road in about 1900, it is impossible to see the prison from the bottom of the bank.

Beacall's Lane, *c.* 1936. The name of the lane commemorated a family of butchers who lived in the area for many years. The car is an Essex belonging to Edward Owen the undertaker, who lived at Lancaster House. At the bottom of the street is the Castle Inn and, in the left-hand corner, the travelling crane from the goods yard.

The junction of Albert Street and Victoria Street, 19 January 1906. The fire broke out in a grocery shop run by Mr A. Palin. Railwaymen arrived on the scene first with their hoses, but found that their standards would not fit the town's hydrants. Both the Alliance and Royal Insurance fire brigades were called in, but a great deal of damage was done before the fire was brought under control. Neither Mr Palin nor Mr Robbins, who lived with his family above the shop, was insured.

The Canal Tavern was set up on the banks of the Shrewsbury Canal in about 1820. Being near the canal's terminus it was a very busy area, drawing its customers from passing bargees and people working on the wharf. The photograph, taken in the 1950s, shows that the tavern was still the hub of local life, with landlord Bill Grierson organizing excursions to the seaside. Favourite destinations at this time were New Brighton and Rhyl. Victor Evans is the third man on the right in the trio standing in front of the driver's cab, while his son, Robert, is the fourth child from the right in the front row.

New Park Road, *c.* 1910. This Wesleyan chapel was built on New Park Road, between Beacall's Lane and North Street, in 1837. It also had a Sunday School for 150 scholars. The notice under the window is advertising a men's Bible class to be taken by John Barker, a well-known local Methodist preacher, and author of the book *Shrewsbury Free Churches*.

All Saints', *c.* 1920. The church in North Street towers above the little cottages which surround it. It was built on land bought by a Mr Barclay Owen, who had been influenced while at university by J.H. Newman, who led the Oxford Movement. Services were held in a small tin hut on this site while the new church was being built around it. When the church was completed, the hut was taken down and removed through the front doors. The architect was Edward Haycock, and building took place in 1875–6. It became a parish church in 1883.

The Weir, *c.* 1910. Before the building of the weir in Castlefields, the town often suffered from a polluted river and the associated health risks during long, hot summers. It was constructed between 1910 and 1912.

Castlefields, *c.* 1931. The new Dennis Pump Escape was demonstrated to the Watch Committee on the riverside by the Welsh Bridge in May 1931. The appliance was purchased through Wales and Edwards and cost £915. This photograph was taken at the end of New Park Road. The houses on the left are by New Park Close.

Dorset Farm, *c.* 1940. The farm, and later Dorset Street, both take their name from Dorset's Barn. A barn of that name is shown on A. Hitchcock's map of 1832, by the river, near the old towpath.

# THE OUTER
# SUBURBS

*The Sentinel, Whitchurch Road, c. 1925. Early in 1915, the Glasgow firm of Alley and*
*MacLellan bought sixteen acres of land on the west side of Whitchurch Road to build their*
*new factory. Work on the building began in March, and by July of that year the first steam*
*waggon had rolled off the assembly line and was ready for testing. In 1918, the factory*
*became known as the Sentinel Waggon Works, and traded under that name until 1957.*
*The firm's motto was 'Ever watchful, on the alert'.*

These Sentinel lorries, one diesel and one petrol-driven, were exhibited at the 1947–8 Motor Show. The shape of the cab is very similar to the Sentinel Garner, built ten years before. The man on the left is Harry Galliers, the works supervisor, and next to him is Mr Lakelin, the works manager.

Sentinel Gardens, *c*. 1920. Across the road from the factory, a model housing estate was built for the workers and their families. Each house had six rooms as well as a scullery and a bathroom. They also had large gardens, a playing field and other recreation areas.

Whitchurch Road, *c*. 1935. The factory houses on the right were known as Sentinel Gardens. In the early years, the works' powerhouse supplied the houses with electricity, central heating and constant hot water for a small sum deducted from wages.

Just above the factory, in the 1930s, a private housing estate was built by Fletchers. The roads were named after places in the Lake District, and houses could be bought for £495. These shops were built on the main road to cater for the new homes and for the people living in Sentinel Gardens. Arthur Fishwick ran the post office and sweet shop.

This camp was opened on Whitchurch Road during the First World War by the Royal Flying Corps. During the 1920s, it became the RAF Road Transport Depot. Vehicles brought here were tested, painted and despatched to their units all over the world.

Little Harlescott Lane, c. 1925. The Chatwood Safe Co. Ltd moved their head office and factory to Shrewsbury in the 1920s. They chose a site in Harlescott and, opposite their works, built a village with modern homes for their employees. The village is shown on the left-hand side. The Midland Red ran a regular service into town.

St Mary Magdalene Church, Battlefield, *c*. 1930. The Battle of Shrewsbury took place in 1406. After the defeat of the rebels, Henry IV ordered that a church should be built on the site and prayers offered up daily for all who had died in the battle. The building was ready in 1409, and a college with eight chaplains established the following year.

Sundorne Castle, *c*. 1930. The castle was built at the beginning of the nineteenth century and belonged to the Corbett family. Even though it was scheduled as a building of historical and architectural importance, it was demolished in September 1955.

Uffington Ferry, *c*. 1910. Ferryman Alan Davies and his family pose proudly for the photographer, Arthur Knight. In the background are Ferry Cottages. The ferry provided a direct route from Monkmoor to Uffington, and was in regular use until 1950. The last ferryman was Will Stephens.

The Shrewsbury Canal, *c*. 1920. The canal was officially opened in 1797, and for many years only provided a link between the county town and the east Shropshire coalfield. This photograph was taken in 1920 and shows Mrs Downer sitting on a bridge over the canal between Berwick Wharf and Uffington.

Sutton Farm and Mill, *c*. 1950. A mill on this site was first recorded in 1144, when Ivo Pantulf of Wem gave it to Shrewsbury Abbey. After the dissolution, the mill was bought by the Mackworth family, who were responsible for building the first stone mill. In about 1786, two mills were built on this site to grind corn. During the nineteenth century, one of the mills was adapted to grind barytes, a compound of barium used in the manufacture of paint, paper and fabrics. From about 1930, the farm was occupied by Mr Yates and his family. Mr Yates reared mainly beef cattle, but he also had a small dairy herd and a milk round in Belle Vue and the Back of the Sheds.

Bayston Hill, *c.* 1910. Bayston Hill lies 2½ miles south of Shrewsbury on the Shrewsbury–Hereford road. On the left is the main village shop. The boys on the left are standing outside the home of Charles Howells, a beer retailer. The site was redeveloped into the Three Fishes Inn.

The Windmill, Lyth Hill, *c.* 1904. Built by John Carter in 1835, the mill was used for processing hemp and flax fibres for rope-making. The mill worked up until this century, but, in 1920, the owner, Mr Hayway, removed both the machinery and sails.

Meole Brace Church, 1934. The Mayor of Shrewsbury, Mr Richard Mansell, is entering the church for the first civic service in Meole. In May 1934, Meole Brace was officially incorporated into the town and, at the service, the mayor thanked the people of Meole for their hospitality and welcomed them into the borough. Standing by the door is Chief Constable Frank Davies.

The Ice Factory, *c.* 1920. A water mill had occupied this site for several hundred years. It was converted in about 1912. Ice was manufactured from pure spring water, and the firm was patronized by the local nobility, gentry, butchers and fishmongers.

Shrewsbury bypass was opened by the Princess Royal on 23 May 1933. The new bridge over the Rea Brook was built of ferro-concrete and replaced an old cast-iron bridge designed by Thomas Telford. On the left is the Brooklands Hotel.

Meole Brace, *c.* 1907. These premises belonged to Edwin Williams, the local blacksmith. The forge stood just below the last cottages on Lower Road going out of town. Mr Williams took the business over from Joseph Holdbrook in about 1900. Standing in the gateway are Mr Williams and his apprentice.

Radbrook College, *c.* 1910. The official title for the college, which opened in 1901, was the Shropshire Technical School for Girls. It was situated on a ten acre site with its own playing fields, tennis courts and gardens. It had accommodation in the early years for fifty boarders, each having a separate bedroom.

In 1901, the course of instruction was intended to prepare students to become efficient heads of households or for practising a branch of domestic science as a means to a livelihood. The school later became a teacher training college for domestic science and rural studies.

The Grapes, Bicton Heath, c. 1910. This is a very old public house, and it was known in 1774 as the Bunch of Grapes. It was demolished in May 1936, and the new inn was built on the same site. It used to sell Lichfield Ales.

The town's new waterworks were opened at Shelton in July 1935. The ceremony was performed by Viscountess Bridgeman. Photographed in the foreground, left to right, are: Mr Beddard, the Revd E.M. Darling, Mrs Cock, the mayor, Lady Bridgeman, and Mr Prideaux, the town clerk. The water tower was known locally as 'Beddard's Pork Pie'.

# FLOODS

*The Welsh Bridge, c. 1946. The older suburbs of the town have always been badly affected by floods. In the middle of the nineteenth century, an old Salopian wrote this verse to record the cause of many a flood in the town: 'When rain comes instead of snows, / Fast as it comes, so fast it goes. / But when comes snow instead of rain, / The waters with us now remain. / Then rain and thaw can bode no good, / For both together make the flood'.*

Frankwell, *c*. 1946. People wishing to cross from the town into Frankwell had to negotiate the floods twice, as both approaches to the bridge were under water. At peak times, pedestrians often had to queue to pass over the planks.

Frankwell, *c*. 1877. The house immediately behind the coach is the Fox public house, run by R. Richards, an ale and porter merchant. Even in these conditions, the men of Frankwell would be conveyed by boat or coach and enter through an upper window to obtain their favourite beverages.

Frankwell, *c.* 1925. Coracles were a common sight in Frankwell, and were put to very good use, ferrying people and provisions to places ordinary boats could not reach. During one flood, Neddy Powell carried himself, a boy, a hundredweight of coal and a gallon of water to his marooned house by the Barge Gutter.

Frankwell Quay, *c.* 1941. According to local folklore, when the Severn rises to the height of the dolphin's mouth on the English Bridge, the water begins to seep into the suburbs. Water always enters the Little Boro' through a drain on the quay known as the 'Frankwell Thermometer'.

Frankwell, 1899. The gentlemen's urinal is completely surrounded by water, and several men attempt to get to their homes up one of the many narrow courts on the quay. During these floods, the corporation was praised for its promptness in putting out temporary walks. In Frankwell, the plank bridge was erected under the direction of the borough surveyor, but turned out to be of such a rickety nature that several people slipped off it on the Monday and had a ducking.

Frankwell, 1947. The Severn started rising rapidly on Monday 18 March, and continued to rise until midday on the Thursday, when it reached its peak of just over 19 ft, at which it remained for seven hours. Flood wardens went into action for the first time during this flood and saved a lot of people a great deal of hardship by removing furniture to safety before the water could spoil it.

Frankwell, *c*. 1960. On 5 December 1960, the Severn burst into over 500 houses, shops and business premises when it reached a peak of 18 ft 5 in. Removal firms moved furniture into two main storage depots. Coleham School and the Public Baths. After the flood had receded, six clean-up groups assembled. Each group consisted of one borough engineer, a flood warden, a pump manned by fire service personnel, an RAF hot-air dryer manned by the men from Shawbury, and a party of boys from the Priory Boys School with buckets, mops and brooms.

Chester Street, *c.* 1925. In 1853 William Ranger conducted an enquiry into the sanitary conditions of Shrewsbury. He suggested that, to alleviate flooding, a canal should be cut from Coton Hill 'of sufficient depth and width to carry away all surplus water from the town and deliver it 2,500 yd below the English Bridge'. Standing in the flood is Richard Henry Croft.

Castle Foregate, *c.* 1947. The flood of February 1947 was one of the highest in living memory. The water in Castle Foregate reached almost as far as the Plough. People from St Michael's Street could only reach the town via Castlefields and the Dana.

Chester Street, *c.* 1947. With so many people trapped in the upper floors of their houses, it was extremely difficult to supply them with their daily needs. Local milkman Fred Jones, sitting in the front of the kayak, would row round the flooded areas, stand on top of railings and climb ladders to make sure his customers got their daily pint of milk.

Castle Walk, *c.* 1947. Both approaches to the bridge were cut off by water. Although only inches deep on the Underdale side, it brought its own dangers. The council workman is sweeping away the silt which caused a number of cyclists to slip off their bicycles.

Coleham Head, *c.* 1928. The area where the Rea Brook joins the Severn is always badly affected. During the flood of 1795, the bridge that crossed the Rea at this point was washed away.

Coleham Head, *c.* 1928. The landlord of the Swan lays out planks for his customers for the last time. The inn was de-licensed in June 1928, and demolished for road-widening and shops.

Longden Coleham, *c.* 1947. Several feet of water affected houses on both sides of Longden Coleham and stretched beyond the Crown Inn. The river also affected the freezing plant at the Kings Hall cinema, so local schoolchildren were treated to free ice-creams.

Longden Coleham, *c.* 1947. This flood badly affected the shops of Mrs Mound, Mrs Allen and Rowlands. Notice the depth of water on the wheels of the cart. The dray belonged to the Corona factory, the horse was called Happy and the driver was Albert Jones.

Abbey Foregate, *c.* 1869. The Severn, during this flood, which occurred just five days before Christmas, rose to a height of 19 ft 4 in. One gentleman who lived to the north of The Abbey used to beat the floods by taking out two chairs with him. By moving from one chair to the other, he managed to move around well, although progress was slow.

Abbey Foregate, *c.* 1946. This photograph can be dated by the air raid shelter in the front of the church. As well as council punts, army vehicles were used during this flood to ferry pedestrians up and down the Foregate.

Shrewsbury Abbey, *c.* 1947. The church has always been badly affected by the floods, as this account from a 1795 *Chronicle* reveals: 'The graves inside the church are sunk in so much that the gravestones are all thrown out of their places. The ends of many of them fallen in and the other ends standing above ground, which makes a most awful and striking appearance and puts us in mind of the general resurrection when it is said "the graves shall give up their dead".' Rowing the boat is the Revd M.L.A. Wilkinson; on the left is churchwarden Sid Morris.

Abbey Foregate, *c.* 1946. Several inches of water managed to get into the Park Hotel on this occasion. The lady demonstrates the difficulties of entering property surrounded by water.

Abbey Foregate, *c.* 1946. During the floods of 1946–7, the water almost completely surrounded the church. Visitors can gauge the height of the water inside the church by the slight discoloration of the wood on the lower portions of the nave pews.

# Acknowledgements

As in my first book, the photographs in this volume are taken from my collection of slides and photographs built up over the past twenty years. Once again I am grateful to so many people for their kindness and generosity in trusting me with their photographic treasures. In particular, I would like to thank those listed below for items used in this book:

Abbeycolor • Mr P. Bebbington • Mr S. Benger • Mr W. Brown
Mr and Mrs W. Caswell • Mr M. Causer • Mr and Mrs I. Davies • Miss B. Downer
Mr R. Evans  Miss D. Galliers • Mr G. Galliers • Mr R. Hands
Mr and Mrs D. Harris • Mr F. Heath • Mrs Hepworth • Mrs C. Hole • Mrs L. Horler
Mr P. Hughes • Mrs F. Jones • Mr J. Kelsall • Local Studies Library
Mrs M. Medlicott • Mrs M. Moran • Mr D. Morris • Mrs E. Morris
Mrs J. Mumford • Mr G.A. Parfitt • Mr and Mrs J. Powell • Mrs E. Ruscoe
Mrs M. Thomas • Mr N. Turner • Mr D. Walley • Mrs K. Williams
Mrs J. Woodhouse • Mrs S. Wynne

I would like to express my thanks to Tony Carr and his staff at the Shropshire Record and Research Centre for their continued help and friendly advice. I am also grateful to the following people for sharing their memories and local knowledge with me, as this has helped enrich the text and bring the photographs alive:

Mr M. Causer • Mr H. Corfield • Mr R. Hughes • Mr G.A. Parfitt • Mr J. Powell
Mrs R. Trumper • Mr N. Turner

I am indebted to Mr Robert Evans of Abbeycolor for his technical advice in preparing the photographs for publication, and to my wife Wendy for all her hard work at the keyboard.

# Bibliography

B. Champion, *Everyday Life in Tudor Shrewsbury*, Shropshire Books, 1994
D. Cromarty, *Everyday Life in Medieval Shrewsbury*, Shropshire Books, 1991
H.E. Forrest, *Old Houses in Shrewsbury*, Wildings, 1920
J.L. Hobbs, *Shrewsbury Street Names*, Wildings, 1954
T. Howell, *A Stranger in Shrewsbury*, J. Watton, 1816
L.C. Lloyd, *The Inns of Shrewsbury*, Shrewsbury Circular, 1942
J.B. Oldham, *A History of Shrewsbury School*, Basil Blackwell, Oxford, 1952
B. Trinder (ed.), *Victorian Shrewsbury*, Shropshire Libraries, 1984

# BRITAIN IN OLD PHOTOGRAPHS

To order any of these titles please telephone Littlehampton Book Services on 01903 721596